AF229662

i
will
write
LOUDLY
so you
can
hear
me
karyn m. bruce

Copyright 2018 Karyn M. Bruce
All rights reserved.

No part of this publication may be reproduced, in any form or by
any means, without the prior permission in writing, except for brief
passages in a published review.

CreateSpace
Paperback ISBN-10: 1986847225
ISBN-13:978-1986847223

Editor: Matthew Lippman
Cover Design: Melissa Stevens
www.theillustratedauthor.net

Selected poems in this book have previously appeared in *America at
the Millennium* and *The Ann Arbor Review*. Pictures used are the sole
property of the author.

contents

part one

part two

I grew up in the 40s and 50s, when child abuse was more common than many people cared to believe. In my case, the alcoholism of my parents had a direct and profound effect on me both physically and emotionally. They fought far beyond the verbiage; they attacked each other, and at many times, I was caught in the middle. When one was mad at the other, they were also mad at me. "You are just like your mother" or "You are just like your father." I had to learn how to bounce from really happy moments to the worst anyone can imagine. What I saw, what I heard, what I grew up with, left many unseen scars.

In 1978 when the novel *Mommy Dearest* was published and Joan Crawford was exposed as an abusive mother, the book was a shocker because, like all the other "me, too" situations, child abuse was also not talked about. It was a secret. As was mine. While all my neighbors knew about the drinking and yelling and fighting, I don't think they really understood, or wanted to understand, what I actually went through. While they felt sorry for me, they didn't want to put themselves or their own families in the middle or someone else's problems.

This book is about my survival, physically and emotionally. The writing has not been easy, and remembering the past, as it really was, has taken me to places I never wanted to re-visit. Some of the poems might be difficult for you to read, much less understand. But there are other moments, moments filled with awareness and joy. I remember them, too, and celebrate them because they also shaped me into who I am today. And I happen to like her.

It is a shame that my mother (most of all) or my father did not have the opportunity to know me. My mother died when I was 21 of cirrhosis of the liver. My father, always in love with the memory of who my mother once was, expected me to grow up to "be" her, or as he would say, "if you could be half the person your mother was." He died when he was 67, still waiting.

While I love most poetry, the poets who have had the most influence on the way I see everything have been Lawrence Ferlinghetti, e.e.cummings, Theodore Roethke, Donald Hall, Jane Kenyon, and Anne Sexton. Their images and words rock my world, and have for almost six decades! Like the power of a scar. "One that would show."

preface

Karyn M. Bruce's *I WILL WRITE LOUDLY SO YOU CAN
HEAR ME* is a quiet book. It's a book of poetry that takes all of
the tendrils of the human experience and wraps them together
in a way that is soft and full and will send you to a place deep in
your own heart, so that when you arrive there, you will feel like
you have discovered yourself all over again, and, then, for the
first time. These poems are big and small because Bruce's work is
so particular. You feel as if the experiences she writes about are
your own. This is a testament to the generosity of the language
and the manner in which it holds and contorts—contorts in a
way that is mesmerizing and quiet, an orchid of poetry. This
book is so quiet you can hear it from a hundred miles away. This
book has such a hush that it echoes in the chambers of the day,
long after the poems have been read. What a gift.

In Bruce's poem, "July, 1969", Bruce opens, "The shortest
poem in the world/is the one that fits neatly inside a whisky
bottle." This is the kind of visionary sprinkle and froth that
exists in these pieces. What an opening and how true. Lines,
as such, allow the reader to feel Bruce's imaginative spirit.
The short poem, like bathed in bourbon, tethered and sunk
in that amber hue? What a great image. Delicious, really. It's
that quiet and then, the quiet of "The Need For Words." She
writes, "My father taught me about the stars/on autumn nights
when we would sit outside/with our cocker-spaniel and look for

constellations." The meditation on childhood and tenderness is that heartwarming heartbreak that makes everything authentic and fantastic. Every poem begins anew. Every poem asks the reader to join the narrative and experience it, and so there is a generosity of spirit which is irresistible. What more could you want from a poem then to be held? The poems in this book do that, like a mother, a friend, a lover, a world. They embrace like a whole world and you can feel a solidarity with quiet, with love and pain, and the exploration of anger and forgiveness.

One of my favorite poems in this collection is "Perhaps You Do Not Remember." Bruce begins by writing,

what a nasty child I was to spew
profanities from a porch-made-cage at you,
your parents! Oh what rage
entangled me so young as this
to hate the love that others knew?

What strikes me about Bruce's work is her ability to get right to the heart of the matter in a way that is honest. She is not messing around, and, in her not messing around, there is an intelligence that is universal and magnanimous. This is exaltation. It is celebration of a life, specifically, and yet when you read these words you can say, "Yes, I know this. This feels familiar and earnest." It's that quiet shout of the human buzz and, for me, I can say, "I most certainly remember." This is why I love this poem, why I love all of these poems, because they make me remember things that I thought I might have misplaced in the memory bank of my own mind. But, no, here they are in the center of these poems, these instances of rage and bravery, of love and sweetness, of the kind quiet that comes with living a full life.

I WILL WRITE LOUDLY SO YOU CAN HEAR ME is an extraordinary book for its own sense of worth. These are confident and sturdy poems. They know themselves. They are comfortable in their own skin. They don't play games. Bruce is a poet of incredible range and you can feel that range on every page. She wants you to brandish your flowers and your teapots and your rakes and your harmonies. She wants you to hold them all very close because, as a poet, she does this in all of her things, especially her own "big, messy crinkled up head." The truth is, we all have big and messy heads. Bruce's beauty is that from that messiness she has made this tumultuous and quiet beauty of a book. I have been listening to it for a long time and I am happy to say that I can hear them, in the quiet hum of the day. They whisper to me like flowers, and I listen with my whole being.

Matthew Lippman

a whole bunch of thanks

There are many people who deserve acknowledgement and to whom I am deeply grateful for being a huge part of my life. My life has been shaped by their presence in it, and they just make me happy.

I would like to thank *Phyllis*, my friend since Kindergarten, who wrote poems, played the violin, and shared her God with me (I "inherited" two out of the three from you); *FFW* who has always believed in my talents and pushed me to write more and more and more; *Richard Messer*, my creative writing professor/advisor/friend at Bowling Green State University, and along with becoming a better writer, I learned from him to appreciate oatmeal with a cold glass of champagne; *Alicia and Mary* were my best friends, my next door neighbors, my playmates, my enemies, my companions walking to school, who had me believing for a very long time that there really was such a place as Sunshine Mountain; *Barbara* and *Judy*, have been my friends for over 44 years. I do not know how I could have managed my life without you both being in it with all our good times, bad times, and all the craziness woven into them. It's good that you are still a phone call, or airplane ticket, away. I will always need you and want you in my life.

And, while my husband, *Steven*, is not a saint, he does possess saintly qualities, an adventurous spirit, and the ability to make me feel special, loved, needed. If I haven't said thank you enough, here's one more: Thank you!

And, a special "thank you" goes to *Matthew Lippman*, a poet and teacher, who has offered so much of his time and expertise to help me grow as a poet, and whose encouragement made this book possible.

for
Cathryn, my daughter
and
my granddaughter, Anna Grace

I Will Write Loudly So You Can Hear Me

for my daughter, Cathryn

Watching you in this place of tears
I am reminded
of other women
and the sound that memories make
when left alone too long.

Here in my kitchen
I plant herbs in window pots
teas and ointments
to soothe old wounds
and dreams.

I have inherited the family album
this womb fomented
with oil and prayers to lessen the pain.

Mother/daughter/mother
the bonds between us
entangle us in shadows.

I will write loudly so you can hear me.
It is January
and I am forcing dandelions to breathe.

part one

karyn m. bruce

I Was Never Allowed to Attend Funerals

not when my Grandma died,
or my Aunt Donna, or my Nono.
I was left behind with nurses or babysitters.
When Nono and Aunt Donna died in the same week
I was sent to Alicia's house.
I lost my tooth there, and my childhood.
She told me there was no such thing as a Tooth Fairy
and showed me my hidden-in-the-dish-cabinet-tooth.
I found out where babies came from
how to ride a bike
and that Santa Claus and the Easter Bunny
were lies our parents told us.

I never really missed my dead relatives.
One day they were there, the next they were gone.
My mom and dad stopped crying.
The end.
The first funeral I attended was my mother's.

I was twenty-one. My father had a mental breakdown.
No aunts. No uncles. No cousins. They all deserted me.
Accused me of killing my mother. Causing her to drink.
I found out what clichés were.
"She's at peace now" and "don't cry" "everything will be ok."
Stupid things people say when there isn't anything to say.

After the cemetery rituals
I went home and dumped the whiskey bottles
she had buried in old, musty-smelling suitcases.
That was the only funeral that made any sense.

karyn m. bruce

In Perfect Black & White

The first time I saw you in a photo
you had one foot on the running board of a 1928 Ford.
Your hair, frizzing all over your head, you were frowning
at the camera. That other picture of you at fifteen
in a tutu-arabesque-pose. You told me how you taught yourself
ballet, how a couple from England wanted to adopt you
to put you in their troupe. But Nona wouldn't sign the paper.
So there you were, stuck in that photo on your toes.

There were pictures of aunts, uncles, and cousins.
At spaghetti dinners. Out at Morgan's Woods playing banjos
and accordions. Polka skirts twirling on a wooden floor.
Those photos of everyone in bathing suits at Goguac Lake
posed pageant-style in bathing caps and foamy waves.
There were the weddings and baptisms and holiday shots
and your mother and father out by the grapevines
or sitting on the back porch steps. Without smiles.

There were hundreds of photos of you,
shiny with girlfriends and boyfriends in jalopies and bars
full of lipstick and nail polish. Even in black & white

I could pretend the colors you were wearing
as you waved out from the Savings Bond float
doing your part to help with the war.

You showed me photos of old boyfriends and your dog, Tootsie,
the one who hated Daddy and bit him when you were dating.
Photos of you in lounging pajamas. Evening gowns.
Sparkly dresses. Big hats. Lacy blouses.

All those afternoons of mother and daughter
we were tucked into each other
my head under your chin, your voice slipping through my hair.
In perfect black & white.

karyn m. bruce

July, 1969

The shortest poem in the world
is the one that fits neatly inside a whiskey bottle
and sloshes around, fermenting there in smoky, sweet amber.
The one my mother never read.
Not the one she wrote for me once when I got a job
at the Enquirer & News "Youth Page" in seventh grade
about a snowman because I could not think of any words
to fill up the page.
That was the only poem *she* wrote, the only one *she* read.
It fit neatly on the printed page
with my name across the bottom.
She never saw the one I entered into a contest
in eighth grade, the one the nuns loved
because it was about Jesus and hanging on the cross.
I knew a lot on that subject.
How he called out for help and no one came
because everyone was asleep. That was the shortest poem.
And it won first place. On both counts.

The shortest poem. Like life. Poof! We're gone.
Just like that when we least expect it.
Unless we are 90-years-old and all our relatives and friends
are already dead. Then we have a short-poem-funeral.
Cheap. Simple. Empty. Not like my mother's.
The funeral director had to open up two rooms
for the rosary. The church was half full for the Mass.
I don't remember what the priest said.
It had to be short. What could he say? She was a drunk?
She was thrown out of the car at 3 a.m. when her cronies
got tired of her? She didn't remember her daughter in the end?
Just like that. The shortest poem. I didn't. Exist.
I don't write short poems. Not like Ezra Pound. Or Hallmark.
I am not a compact person.
Only once. On my mother's grave stone. Those two lines.
Without my name.

karyn m. bruce

The Need for Words

My father taught me about the stars
on autumn nights when we would sit outside
with our cocker-spaniel and look for constellations.
He would point to the Big Dipper, Orion,
often Taurus, my zodiac sign.
On rare occasions,
we would see the Goodyear blimp floating by,
flashing its Goodyear advertisement
for everyone to read.

He bought a book about birds.
Together we would explore the birdfeeder
hanging in the backyard apple tree
and expertly find birds on those colorful pages.
The day we saw an albino robin, we called
Kingman Museum, and we took a picture of it because
it wasn't in the book.

I never saw my father read a real book
only *Argosy* magazine and the *Enquirer & News,*

but he forced me to read books each summer,
dumb books I shoved under my bed
to return to Willard Library in two weeks, untouched.

He made box kites from scratch for us each spring
without reading any directions
using his old boxer shorts fabric for the tails.
They flew a hundred miles into the air
while we sat on the hill and ate our paper bag lunches.

He liked to laugh.
He liked to make others laugh.
He taught himself how to make balloon animals
by following the directions on the balloon box
so that he could go to the Children's Home
and watch the little kids giggle and clap their hands
and he would entertain all my friends at my birthday parties.

He died in March 1983
and lay quiet in his casket for two days
while friends and relatives passed by, nodding,
praying, whispering, engrossed in the guest book,
reading who had visited, and, perhaps, who had not.

He'd always have an inside joke, some remark
about people who'd show up to "the main event"
like my wedding, my mother's funeral, his retirement,
but were never in our lives, actually.
I could just hear him asking me from his front row position
"Why are *they* here?" like he had done
while he was dying in the hospital
when people made their daily visits to appease their guilt.

When I looked for a suit in his closet
in which to bury him
I found that gigantic "Kiss Me, I'm Irish" pin,
the one he wore every St. Patrick's day.
I wanted to pin it on him. Almost did.
He would have liked that. And it made me laugh
to think what this crowd of spectators
would have read into *that*,
especially since he wasn't Irish.

It was enough
that I had a Catholic priest read the eulogy
and bring red balloons to his grave.

I read a poem there, too,
one that I had written about him and he liked.
We sent those red balloons up into the March sky
just like his famous kites, while we stood
in the snow-covered grass, to read the final Amen.

karyn m. bruce

Lizzie Borden Took An Axe

Summers were better than winters.
I didn't need shoes or a coat
to run to the neighbor's house
to call an ambulance
when my father hit my mother.
But one winter day I ran barefoot
all the way to the end
of our street
dressed only in her blood
because I tried to stop her dying
all by myself.

Lizzie Borden took an axe

My father's hands were around her throat,
Her body pushed up against the wall.
I hit him....I hit him hard.
He yelled, "get out of here!"
and smacked my face

and chased me around the house.
At least my mother got away.

Lizzie Borden took an axe

When I was older, my best friend called me a tramp.
She told me that the only reason
I had friends at all was because
they felt sorry for me because of my parents.
My godmother told my parents
that if I grew up like them
it would be their fault and that was unfortunate.

Lizzie Borden took an axe

The night my mother locked my father
out of the house
my father refused to come inside
when I opened the door.
He said it had to be my mother.
And she wouldn't.
And I wouldn't leave the kitchen.

With an old piece of telephone pole
my father rammed the back door.
Glass splintered across my face.

Lizzie Borden took an axe

On those nights
when I had to be in the car with her
I'd hide on the floorboard of the back seat.
The stench of alcohol and the weaving of the car
made me dizzy and I'd dig my nails
into the carpet until I'd ripped it open.
She never knew
that was where I memorized my prayers;
that was where I disappeared into a scream.

Lizzie Borden took an axe

Good for you, Lizzie.

Baseball 101

I spent most summer afternoons
sitting in the living room with my dad
as he watched the Detroit Tigers
from his over-stuffed, orange chair.
I slurped my pop from the couch
and waited for that last sip of his Stroh's beer
no longer cold, but his.

Once a month, we went down to Bailey Park
to watch the Battle Creek City team
where I did not mind a ball careening into the open stands
or dirt on my hot dog. I wasn't even embarrassed
when he hollered the runner was "safe" at home plate
or at the other team's pitcher
with his paper-cup beer spilling over the sides.

It was in front of the black & white television
where he'd try to teach me the plays, told me what to look for
when Al Kaline was up to bat or Jim Bunning was pitching.

karyn m. bruce

One summer he stopped rooting for the Tigers
and sported a red and white Cubs' cap.
Nothing else changed.

I went to major league games after his death
wearing any one of his worn out caps
and screaming at the top of my lungs.
It didn't matter what team was winning
or even where I sat.
It was the barking of vendors, "Pop corn. Peanuts,
get'cha ice cold beer" and all the people
jam-packed into the stands
hoping to catch that fly ball slicing through the heat
into the last swig of summer.

What Summer Painted Us

The dry-brown August air filled our lungs
as we played Cowboys and Indians or dared each other
to swing the highest or jump out splayed and sprawled
up and over the afternoon.
We would climb the apple tree, or play hide-and-seek
until someone made it "home."
We drank Kool-Aid from wash tubs filled with ice
our parents put out under the tree in Mary's yard,
or hid in the Standish's grapevines, our mouths and fingers
tell-tale purple. We'd play dress-up with our dolls
or we'd build hideouts in the vacant lot of sumac trees.
Through the years, we learned to skate, ride bikes,
bring our dimes to the lady on Vineyard Street
who made ice cream.
We'd pretend we were the Lil' Rascals and make up shows
for no one else to see.

karyn m. bruce

Defining Awkward

According to my father, my mother could dance
as good as Ginger Rogers.
When he was in the Army, she followed him
one town to the next, dancing the nights away
in all those glitzy juke joints.

I was five-years-old when
she enrolled me in tap dancing class.
I loved the sound of my patent leather shoes
tapping out my shuffle-step
in front of the studio mirror with the other girls.
I wanted to look like Shirley Temple
from the movies my mother made me watch.
I waited and waited after each class
hoping this time she would smile.

I danced with my father only once.
He left me standing alone in the middle of a song

with his loud, "You can't dance like your mother"
while everyone else swirled around me, a catastrophe
of eyes and rhythm, meshing into the last note of nothing.

I cried against my mother's casket at the cemetery.
Later, at the family gathering, I overheard my uncle tell my father
that everyone would have been okay. If I hadn't.

karyn m. bruce

My Mother Took Me to the YMCA

for swimming lessons
when I was nine
because she was afraid I would drown
in Goguac Lake, the only place
anyone in Battle Creek could swim for free.
That, in itself, was the most stupid of ideas
because in all my years
we had never gone swimming there
or anywhere.
So, I spent twelve weeks paddling my way
through beginners' to intermediate
and almost drowned once when
I slipped beneath the surface
and did a half-somersault
on the bottom of the pool.
I finished every required stroke that summer
without dipping one toe in the lake.

When my friends asked if I could go swimming
my parents said I'd have to wait for them to take me.
And that was the second most stupid thing
I ever heard in my life because my parents
didn't *ever* have time to take me *anywhere.*
Unless it was their idea.
I grew up like that with the stupidest things.
I wasn't allowed to ride a bike
because my mother was afraid I'd fall off
or get killed by a phantom car
that on rare occasions would appear on our dirt road.
My friends taught me in secret and my mother
never would have known except that one day
I fell off Sally's bike and fainted.
No one could have covered up the purple bruise
where I made contact with the sidewalk.
My dad finally bought me a bike
the summer I took driver's education.
And *that* was the third most stupid thing ever!

It was embarrassing that everyone in the North
knew how to ice skate. I didn't.

That would require going out on
frozen water and sinking beneath the ice
like all those kids my mom told me about
from the evening news, every winter day.

When my daughter was three
we both learned how to ice skate
and I let her take horse-back riding lessons
in our backyard. She fell off once.
And lived to tell everyone.

The Triple X Bar

After school, when B.F. Sherman Manufacturing Co.
released its second shift employees,
my mother and I arrived to meet
Josephine, the red-headed woman
with sagging breasts and stale Emeraude perfume,
who walked up the sidewalk
to the neon-lit bar.
My mother's only friend by then.

She spoke of piece work
relentless foremen and owners
left over from a war or two
only retiring after death had already
seeped into their bones.

Years before, my mother could have told her own stories
of the Michigan Express Trucking Company
and all the men who loaded and unloaded the freight
and secretly loved her.

karyn m. bruce

But now, she could only listen.
One more beer, one more cigarette
another coke for me,
as hours drifted into hours and sloppy smiles.

I did my homework there on the same table
where the beer sloshed over the glasses
and into their laughter, sometimes on my uniform.
When the place had fewer customers, the bartender
taught me how to play shuffleboard and bumper pool.
When there were too many, I was given
red, juke box quarters to play the music for free
anything by Elvis and Pat Boone.

Once in a while my mother's friends bought me
one of those dolls that sat in boxes
on the ledge above the hundreds of liquor bottles,
dressed in frilly dresses and pink, Cupie-doll smiles.

We never sat at the bar
because it was against the law for children

but I grew up there, night after night
getting A's on my homework
and giving A's to myself
for making it to the bathroom and back alone
down the dim-lit hallway
passed the slurry eyes of shadowed voices
whispering, "come here little lady."
I could always hear them watching me
even later, when my mother no longer remembered
where we had been.

karyn m. bruce

What Happens When the Boogeyman Comes?

You left me alone so many times after Daddy went to work and I never wanted to go with you when you walked the dark streets to the store to get booze and cigarettes because I was afraid the Boogeyman would grab us and turn us into the pieces of words that you told me in stories when you were drunk and I never knew what they meant and that made them darker when the moon was falling into the bedroom and I was shaking scared. Like the night I saw him outside the window on the other side of the screen and then the night his shadow filled up the bedroom when the lights were out and I could hear you and that other man laughing and drinking in the living room and you thought I slept through that but I never told Daddy because he would have bashed you into the wall. But those nights you left me alone and I thought I could be brave but I wasn't and I stayed behind the chair in the living room with the butcher knife waiting for the tapping on the door and I cried so hard I peed my pants every time until you came home and I put the knife away and never told you. Not even about those nights when the wind crept up

45

against the house like scratching fingers and I couldn't breathe because it was dark and I was alone and I knew it was too late and why would you ever tell me stories that left me screaming deep inside in that darkest place because …

shhh…he might hear you…never coming home.

karyn m. bruce

The House on Beglin Court, 1940-2014

The house is gone. Burned up in a fire.
It was seventy-four years old.
You-who-torched-it didn't know that.
Never knew it was a home. Where I used to live.
Where things happened.

You ended me. Everything I was.
My finger paintings that seeped into the walls,
my first steps, first words.
The "Gunsmoke" Friday nights with popcorn
and "Ponderosa" Sundays.
The closet over the basement steps where I hid my dolls.
The bedroom corner where I kept my diary.
The birthday parties, the bay window
where I watched for tornadoes every summer,
the room where I wrote my poems.
I have driven by to visit each and every year
to see my mark on the apple tree in the backyard.

You. Whoever you are. Took a match
and disintegrated all those years.
You took a match and watched the flames lick the night sky.
You, Bastard, took a match and made me. Gone.

There is no address now. No mail box.
No sidewalk where I learned to roller skate.
Nothing left that says I was. Here.

Karyn M. Bruce

Indian Givers

Sometimes you just know.
Even if you are three.
One day your mom
will yank your red tricycle
out from under you
and there you are, sitting
on the floor
watching her give your bike
to a red-lipsticked woman,
grabbing at the handle bars.
Even though you hear the words
"She can't afford bikes for her children,
and "you're too big to ride this,"
you know those other kids
shouldn't get yours.
Your mom gave it to you for Christmas.
Your dad created the path in the basement
so you could pedal around and around
when you couldn't ride down the sidewalk.

And there in the shadows of a little tricycle
a memory curls inside you,
and you know nothing will ever be.
Just yours.

karyn m. bruce

On Those Sundays

we ate our breakfast side-by-side,
with the comic section wide open on the kitchen table
both in our pajamas, hair uncombed.
We'd shout together when *Little Orphan Annie* announced
"Leapin' Lizards" and looked out at us with her round,
vacant eyes. Or we'd cry when Sandy, her raggamuffin dog,
was chased by street punks.

Every Sunday *Dick Tracy* saved the day in his yellow detective
hat, while corn-pipe smokin' Mammy Yokum hill-billied
across the page with her "good night Irene punches,"
and Daisy Mae spooned over *Li'l Abner* until he finally
smartened up and married her.

I'd cheer when my mother read *Little Lulu,*
the loopy-curled girl who fought boys and bullies and won,
but never mussed her hair.
And I remember *Brenda Starr* with her long, red waves
and low-cut blouse.

Years later, when I could read the comic strip myself,
I found out that those steamy romances of hers
were never part of my mother's reading.

For each character there was a voice
that swooped and swirled into my ears,
and I would put my finger on top of hers
as she pointed to the words, her red-painted fingernails
gliding into those small bubble-like clouds
above everyone's head.
To my father's displeasure, I would beg her
to read *Dennis the Menace* twice because he loved root beer
and terrorizing babysitters. Just like me.

karyn m. bruce

You Ain't Got Nothin' on the Tiger

Move over, Wheaties!
You ain't got nothin' on the tiger
roaring from the bottom of my cereal bowl.
It doesn't matter how many champions you pose
on that cardboard box. I had Tony
just like almost all the kids in Battle Creek
because most of our parents & grandparents
& aunts & uncles & brothers & sisters worked at Kelloggs!
And we were there to visit almost every school year
since Kindergarten, so we knew first-hand, he was
                    Gr-Gr-Gr-G-R-E-A-T!

My dad was head machinist in the #2 Packing Room
for 42 years, 9 months, & 28 days, and I got all the prizes
packed inside long before any of your baseball players-
Olympian swimmers-&-down-hill-skiers looked out
with their cardboard smiles from the cereal section
of A&P or Kroger's. I don't know what you've got in that box
but I've got Tiger-kicking-ass frosted flakes in mine!

I grew up with the snapping, crackling, poppin' opinion
that anyone who grew up in the Cereal City was better for it!
The first Saturday of summer vacation we all headed for
Michigan Avenue & took our place at that mile-long table
& ate our fill of Kellogg's cereal with lots of cold milk.

My dad always wore his work hat, so that everyone would know
he was a proud employee. When it was over, if us kids
could beat the welfare moms to the left-overs, we brought home
boxes & boxes of single-serving-eat-anytime-flakes.

General Mills, Ralston, Post? They never invited us kids to visit.
Never gave us fresh-hot-roasted-flakes-with-ice-cream
for just walking through their doors. I remember the smell
of Kellogg's cereal roaring through each day of my childhood.
So move over, Breakfast of Champions!
You ain't got nothin' on *this* tiger girl!

karyn m. bruce

When Robert Frost Was the Only Poet

Sitting in wooden desks
in perfectly straight rows
we plotted out
the rhythmic lines
of your poems
our fingers
like tap-dancing feet
across the page.

Our Catholic nuns nodded
in approval
their habits
swinging and swaying
in stanzas
closing their eyes
on the last lyrical period
as if they'd had
an orgasm.

You were the Prophet
of Parables

the only god
of the One True Church
Of Words.

You alone kept us
from falling off the edge
of e.e. cummings'
single parenthesis.

You were the Saint
of the Iambic Pen
while Ferlinghetti
imagined
zig-zagged lines
        until I dizzied
                under the weight
of his voice
        booming from the pages into that
                one, dark space
where I could wait, too,
                for a re-birth of anything
that did not make anyone
redeemed.

karyn m. bruce

Warning: Do Not Use Dick and Jane Books To Teach Children to Read

Every day Dick and Jane jumped out
of the small pages of our books with voices, yelling
"Run, Sally, run!" or *"Sit, Spot, sit."*

Someone should have given them a Medal of Honor
for perfect attendance and for their dedication
all through first grade, each and every year.

There should be a Dick and Jane Museum
somewhere in Nebraska or Arkansas or North Dakota
where we could sit down, once again,
with our miniature glass bottles of milk
to see Puff chase Spot across the page
without the fear of multicultural indiscretion.

Now adults proclaim them
"inappropriate" because they weren't color-coded.

We didn't notice that.
Maybe we would never have noticed that.
We were simply mesmerized by
"Oh, Spot! Look in here!
It is something we like!"
when Sally's blonde-haired, blue-eyed voice
sounded just. like. our. own.

karyn m. bruce

If Robert Bly Remembered the Milkman

I wanted to leap
farther than a tiddlywink
jumping up and over the title
of that poem and around the corner where
the milkman still delivers milk in glass bottles
to the doorstep of every house on the block.

I waited for him all day sometimes
just to get a chunk of ice to suck on.
But it didn't always happen.
Sometimes he was in a bad mood
and there I stood hot and thirsty
wishing I could leap onto that truck
and yank the ice back into my poem
instead of playing with my dolls
who couldn't understand the sophistication
of my anticipation.

Susie

You liked my blinky eyes & my pink-rubber skin,
curly-brown hair & how I said "Mama"
when you pressed my belly.
I loved the pageants in your mother's classy clothes,
tea parties & whispered stories under the covers.
You loved me even after your smelly dog
ran all around the neighborhood
with me in his teeth, ripping out my hair.
You found it later in the yard gnarly & clumped.
It never stuck to the top of my head again.
But you called me pretty.

When I grew older
you wrapped my arms & legs with adhesive tape
month after month, year after year
until the tape became my arms & legs
and my fingers & toes were gone.
You dressed me up in bigger doll clothes & blankets

& took me for walks down the front sidewalk.

I slept on your pillow every night.
You sang lullabies to me & cried on me when you were scared.
I was the only thing no one tried to take from you.
In the end, I was mostly bandages.
You called me yours.

part two

karyn m. bruce

Spring, 1955

It is April. And I am six-years-old.
I can walk to school by myself now.
I know the short-cut through
the small shoots of new grass that line
the beaten down path through the field
made by me and my friends.
It is our path that leads
to the sidewalk on Vineyard Street
straight up to the school.
It is April and I am six-years-old.
Daffodil petals stain the sidewalk
and my socks and shoes as I walk.
My hair dances in the wind.
It is April. And I am six-years-old
and I am walking to school.
The sun swirls into my eyes
and I unbutton my sweater and take it off

63

even though I was told not to
and I feel the warmth on my pale skinny arms.
I am six-years-old and it is April.
For the first time. I know.

karyn m. bruce

Stitches

My mom and I sat in the emergency room
for six hours, waiting for a doctor to come,
and all that time, there were kids screaming
and people throwing up, and shadows of feet
running back and forth and forth and back.
I think someone died although I wasn't sure
because death speaks its own language
and I was only seven-years-old.
At midnight, the doctor came in
and said my knee needed stitches.
He didn't have time to numb it,
he was too busy trying to save lives,
but he brought in five other people to hold me down
so he could jam that needle right through my skin.
All I could do was scream until they stopped holding me
and let me watch the thread weave in and out.
I'd have a scar. One that would show.

How I Got Religion

I knew my Aunt Florence had her work cut out for her
when she set her sights on me, picking me up every Sunday
in her green-rusted-out '55 Ford Fairlane, full of Bibles
and the Matthew, Mark, Luke, and John guys
who spoke in rhythms that made me dizzy.

But I was the chosen one, the one who would save
my parents from the fires of Hell, because she,
born again and again and again, would take me to church
every Sunday to find the "right" Holy Jesus to bring home
and lay at their feet and make everything sanctified.

And I sure saw a lot of pictures of Him.
In every Sunday school room across Battle Creek,
Jesus with sheep, Jesus with a halo,
Jesus with old men in dresses,
Jesus hanging way up there on that cross.
I understood the "Jesus Praying in the Dark" one
because I did that all the time

when my dad and mom had fights and dishes flew
like a church full of "Amens."

Aunt Florence told me anyone could be saved
but sometimes I just wanted it to be the Sunday dinner
that sailed past me out the back door and into the snow.
And Aunt Florence wasn't there when the screaming
was louder than the Hell-raising preacher from Capital Avenue.
I never believed it was the Blood of Jesus splattered across our
living room walls.

But, I was glad someone in my family found " the Lord"
and even though I thought she was perpetually trapped
inside the New Testament in the house of King James,
it all sounded …wholly.
Like a good thing. Like a prayer maybe I could say someday
when I was hiding in the dark closet of my bedroom
trying to save myself.

The First Poem I Ever Created

was a kite I made in sixth grade
a math & science project
on the largest piece of manila paper
precisely cut into a triangle
with folds glued carefully on over string & wood.
I loved my kite.
I loved watching my hands
with my fingernails bitten down to the quick
choosing the perfect crayons for coloring
MY VERY LARGE CAT
across the entire front of the paper.
I remember.
Painstaking strokes.
My fingers
working symmetrical moments
up & over the paper for days.
& days.
& days.

And this kite.
Something I did. By myself.
A smiling cat that would fly away
& swirl to the ground five minutes
after my class went outside.
I didn't even think about crying.
I would remember.
Like the first time I read you, Mr. Eliot,
& found my cat
sitting quietly. Grinning.
On that page.

Beatitudes of a Young Girl

Blessed be the hula-hoop
the ring of plastic filled with weights
that spun on our hips and knees.
I was the first of my friends to own one
and it was my father who brought it home one afternoon.
He even knew how to swing it around his bulging middle
and I laughed so hard I cried right there in the backyard.
My mother thought he was nuts or drunk, pleading
have mercy on us all!

Blessed be pantyhose!
My first pair of nylons had those brown lines
running up the back of my legs like worms,
never staying straight on my legs,
attached to the garter belts that held them in place
with the snaps popping open all the time
against my unwomanly thighs!
Growing up was such a nuisance
with unholy contraptions and thingamajigs!

karyn m. bruce

So praised be Allen Gant who had mercy on us
with his control-top invention,
thus protecting us from a life-time of girdles!

And blessed be Rock 'n Roll, Elvis and his gyrating hips
and Bill Hailey and the Comets and Chubby Checker
do-whopping and be-bopping on the transistor radio
I snuck under my pillow!
My grandmother learned the Twist
and bought a stereo for the 45-speed records,
her neighbors whispering, "Lord, have mercy on us!"

Blessed be the memories
of petticoats, shimmering pink and white lipstick
applied in layers in front of Dianne's mirror
that weekend I slept over,
ponytails, drive-ins, skating rinks, Hosh's Grill,
Catholic school uniform skirts rolled up at the waist,
Dairy Queen, feeding ducks at the Lagoon,
and cruising the gut on Michigan Avenue
on Saturday nights. We were beyond
the prayers of the nuns,

and the priests signing crosses on our foreheads,
and the last Kyrie Eleison sung at Sunday Mass.
Blessed be that almighty forever and ever Amen.

karyn m. bruce

Biology

It began with the pithing,
jamming the long, silver pin
quickly into the space
between its bulging eyes
as it watches me.
It will destroy the brain.
I drop the frog
leave it hopping
across the classroom floor.
I know someone else will do
what I cannot.
Someone else will take the scalpel,
slice through its skin
and pin it in place
to expose its organs.
And its heart will beat
one last time,
drifting like a note of music
through someone else's fingers.
It is relatively painless.

Did I Ever Tell You

73

how much
I loved Saturdays?
Just the two of us
at the kitchen table.
Mother.
Daughter.
Hot pepper sandwiches
and ice-filled glasses
of
cherry Kool-Aide?

karyn m. bruce

Bristol Lake, 1958

My father bought a cabin in Barry County, off M37,
where he tried to sell aluminum rowboats.
Inside, the caved-in roof plunged through cobwebs
strung out like party streamers. Pieces of china dishes
lay on the dingy linoleum floor like a mahjong puzzle,
and remnants of mice poop crunched under our feet.
My mother went back to the car,
but I followed my father down to the lake
and watched him set up the boats.

We came back each month. They were only day trips,
nothing like the real summer vacations all my friends had.
But the lake was deep and dark and beckoning,
and it was on this lake that my father taught me
how to commandeer a rowboat with a motor.

It was there that I saw my first trout, in fact, hundreds
glimmering in a hidden inlet so close to the surface
I could almost touch them,
they unafraid of the shadows we wove through the still water.

And at this lake, my father taught me how to fish.
I'd lay on my stomach, and lean over the side of the dock,
mindful of splinters and rotted wood,
to drop a fishing line into the see-through water below,
cheese balls wrapped around the hook,
where bluegills scooted in the green water weeds,
wiggling away from my longing to catch them.

The cabin, never repaired, was sold years later
and the row boats lined our chain-link backyard fence.
When no one was looking, I used to crawl up inside of them
and make believe we were out on the lake again,
he and I, listening to the jazzy rhythm of the water
lapping against the sides of the boat drifting,
drifting into the frayed edges of a yellow afternoon
where parables live in the songs of fish and fathers.

karyn m. bruce

If You Can Bake Cookies, You Can't Be Too Crazy

When I was very young, I already knew about
the blue "nerve" pills in a crumpled envelope in the credenza,
the white horses that pranced across your room
in that red-bricked hospital on Washington Street.

And I already knew too well what it was like with Nona
falling asleep alone in the musty living room,
headlights from the street creeping across the walls,
watching her bleach the kitchen floor on Mondays
and crochet doilies in the evenings.

Only once did I see you bloated and disfigured
through the rusty bars of the first floor window
your voice slipping away into the peeling wallpaper.
And I held my breath to save for you.

But in July of '69 your room was back in a corner
where the nurses locked up nightmares
and tattered bedspreads.
You no longer babbled about horses.
Or your daughter.

The street is abandoned now, save that building
condemned with its shadows and the stale smell of dreams.
I look at the spaces where the windows once were
and remember the sound of your eyes.

I bake cookies
because you never did.

karyn m. bruce

In Our Twenties, We Smoked Cigarettes
for Barbara

& played gin rummy through the nights when our husbands
worked. We shared food stamps & chicken noodle soup
dinners while my child & her dog slept on the couch.
We both had those "dysfunctional" pasts that we dissected
each evening. Drinking parents, their fights.
When she found out her husband was cheating,
I went with her all over town, looking for him.
We took an entire box of condoms
& threw them over his new girlfriend's car.
When I thought I was pregnant again, she took me
to the free clinic & held me while I cried & cursed God.

We have been friends
for forty-two years, two husbands, & a few lovers.
We survived poverty & fantasies.
We buried our parents, drank rum & cokes
& laughed at the stupid stuff that made us laugh.
We were Thelma & Louise. Bonnie & Clydia.
We never killed anyone

although there were many times when we contemplated it.
When she got cancer, she preferred to have her sisters
who romped around South Haven
& paraded through the hospital
all dolled up for dinners out on the town.

I sent care packages each week with lotions for dried-up skin,
scarves for a balding head, cookbooks with recipes to ease the
nausea & fear. I sent cards to make her laugh: birthday, Bar-
Mitzvah, baby shower. Nothing to remind her she was ill.
It was the closest I could get while she puked up her memories.
We were best friends, I thought.
Her years had filled the spaces in my years.

But I wasn't. A sister.

karyn m. bruce

Perhaps You Do Not Remember

for Mary and Alicia

what a nasty child I was to spew
profanities from a porch-made-cage at you,
your parents! Oh, what rage
entangled me so young as this
to hate the love that others knew?
I, the small child inside the porch-locked view,
spitting words beyond my age,
trapped in what my parents hissed.
What apologies can I now make
to you who suffered, shed your tears,
and shook your heads, for pity's sake?
I was horrid, full of fears
full of vengeance, full of woe.
Please forgive me. I didn't know…
what else to do.

Messy-ness

I have naturally curly hair,
but that wasn't good enough for my mother.
Home perms were the rage when I was six,
and seven, and eight.
And it did not matter if I didn't need one.
I'd have to sit one whole Saturday a month
dipped in perm-stench, my head covered in curlers
to get those perfectly perfect ringlets.

When I turned fourteen, the beauty shops took over.
Then, that last time,
the hair-dresser left the solution on too long
and I went to school with an Afro
which was not the style then, especially on a little white girl.

I had a big, messy crinkled up head.
I was so mad. Furious. Messy.
I let it grow out, til it flared out on my shoulders.
    I began writing messy poems.

82

          I thought messy thoughts
and had messy ideas and a messy life.

      But I got along just fine in my messy world full of
messy words.
I told my mother to fuck off, and the world to fuck off
      as I sat down in the hot-mess
of my own dysfunctional condition.

Summer Burial

Arms cannot show.
Funeral directors will tell you that.
They have to use too much make-up
to cover the dead skin
and your mother will not look natural.
Choose a long-sleeved dress
even if the heat index rises above 100 degrees
and none of the stores have one to sell.
She will not know. She is dead.
And the ground will be cold
even in July.

karyn m. bruce

Things in My Head

I am not like anyone in my family.

My Aunt Marjorie was a poet, too,
but everything I wrote
she attributed to her influence on me
with all the beautiful rhymes she sent me in the mail.

Aunt Donna died too early for me to know who she was
except that she had married a WWII soldier
& then when he was killed
had to come home & live with her mother.
She died just when I thought I had something to say.

Other aunts: the socialite & the housewife.
The uncles: the drinker & the gambler.
My cousins were all boys
except Elizabeth who lived in Arizona
with asthma & Chihuahuas & red hair.

I had a mother who took me to grown-up movies
& we'd eat hot dogs at the counter in Kresge's
where I could twirl around in my seat.
One December she took me Christmas shopping.
The streets were icy & cold & blinked on & off
with colored lights in snowflakes that landed on my face.
She held my hand so I would not fall
& told me all men were bastards.

My father taught me about birds & stars.
He sang silly songs
like "Johnny VerBeck" & "Scotland's Burning."
& showed me
how to make a kite fly a hundred miles into the sky
& how to hurt my mom.

There were two grandmothers:
one from England who served me tea without milk
& never spoke to me
& the grandmother with babushkas
who told me stories full of onions & garlic.

karyn m. bruce

When I was all alone on rainy days
I'd make a tent beside my bed
& spend the afternoons reading to my dolls
while eating bologna sandwiches
& sometimes wondering
about the things in my head

that were not like what anyone had taught me.

Everything About Her

Even after my Nono's death, Nona prepared
the Saturday night spaghetti dinners for the family,
the adults gathering around the dining room table
full of the Old Country lingo, tossed as freely as the salad
and strands of pasta,
the grandchildren huddled together at the kitchen table
dripping with sauce and giggles. Five boys. One girl.
It took her all day to sauté the garlic and onions in butter,
cook the pasta until it stuck to the wall,
chop the tomatoes, the mushrooms, fresh from her garden.
What she did. For her family.

When I was eight, my mother had surgery.
I slept overnight for weeks. She tucked me into flannel sheets
while the sun warmed the sky, and shook me from dreams
when the moon still clung to the living room walls.
She walked me to the hospital to visit my mother, let me
catch tadpoles in a jar at the pond.
What she wanted. For me.

karyn m. bruce

And through the years of weekend visits, we ate breakfast
by the kitchen window. My favorite place.
Eggs, toast, tea with milk and sugar.
Everything filled with the whisper of garlic.
Sometimes we took the bus downtown.
To Ratti's Rummage Sale store where she shopped for skirts
or some shirt-waist for a relative in Italy.
Her upstairs bedroom was full of such items,
on hangers or in boxes.
What she gathered. For her family.

When she could no longer pass me off for a five-year-old,
and the bus ride back to her house became expensive
we walked the two miles through the West End.
It was still morning, but Dairy Queen was open
and she always bought me a kiddy cone.
She told me stories about her mother who died when she
was just three-days-old.
And Nono, working in the coal mines of Calumet
when they first arrived in America.

She told me stories about my mother,
how she married twice before my dad.
She was a wild-child. Ran away from home to Chicago
when she was sixteen. Now her drinking.
Those nights she beat on the front door to steal me away.
How my Nona hid me in her prayers. To keep me safe.

When I was older, I was responsible to write her letters
to the aunts and uncles and cousins in Torino.
Nona would dictate. She told me they wanted
to receive letters in English and would take them
to a man in the village who would translate.
I tried hard to press her voice into every page.

Each day there was always something to do.
She taught me how to use the wringer-washer
and hang the wet clothes out on the line in front of her
garden. She took pictures of me, hiding in the sheets,
my shadows dripping over the grass.
She taught me how to weed the cucumbers and lettuce
and the names of every flower she grew.
We would sit on the front porch steps
and wait for the ice cream boy
to walk down the street in the heat of summer
with his jingle-belled cart of popsicles.
She told me not to be disappointed
if he didn't have cherry because grape was just as good.

karyn m. bruce

She told me to be a good Catholic. A good democrat.
To watch the "stories" of *Love of Life* and *As the World Turns*
every afternoon. How to crochet and stitch Huck towels.
I never asked what she remembered.
Her father, her older sister. Nono. But I always wondered.

She made me laugh with her vocabulary
of "umbershoot" and "babushkas."
She taught me that *West Side Story* had the best sound-track
and the DiMaria sisters were the singing stars in Italy.
We sang all their songs while we did dishes
or dusted the furniture.
She often forgot my mother wouldn't let me learn Italian.
Half-way through a sentence she would correct herself.
And laugh and hug me. And call me "Karina."
It was who she was. For me.

Our Women's Ritual

When I was old enough
we wandered the cemetery streets
looking for your dead friend's & family's graves.
We watered flowers, pulled weeds,
& walked for hours
in & out of your memories.
I always wanted someone to get up & run over
to thank us for coming
or for one of those porcelain photos stuck
on those tombstones
to smile back at us.

It is my duty to brush the family graves free of dead things
& place flowers in the tin pots provided.
I know that the grave diggers might steal them
like Nono did for Nona after his shift was over
& the smell of death walked him home.

Maybe these flowers that I bring
will simply wither in the sun or just drown in the rain.

karyn m. bruce

Maybe a dog will wander through
& pee on them.

I watch the others here, hands on watering cans,
hands in prayers, hands in hands,
hands dripping from tears,
hands with nothing else to do
but arrange & re-arrange the silence.

Just once I wish someone
would rise up from the grave
dancing & singing
because this is such a dead place
& no one wants to be here
& it really would make a perfect spot
for a Morgan's Woods' banjo-playing-picnic.

To the Dead Word Poet's Society

There is nothing pastoral about her.
She can belt out a song
like Ethel Merman or Janis Joplin
or even Pink.
She's a Rosy-the-Riveter, a hell-raising
sweet-fucking-red-headed-there-you-have-it
shot-gun Calamity Jane
whipping-along-to-the-rhythm-in-my-bones.
That bolt of lightning
that wakes up the be-Jesus inside me.

My ass-kicking, word-dancing, sunset-slathered
alter-ego, prayer-kissing, sagacious *soul*
is only dead to you.
Carpe Anima. Breathe.

karyn m. bruce

Sleeping With Sunflowers
for Judy

I bought clay pots that September
& planted sunflower seeds inside the warm dirt
watching them grow into small shoots
bending toward the sunlight
from the window sill.

In my mind I have created a room,
above the clatter of voices,
filled with flowers & pieces of paper
scattered across a red wooden table
where my cats will sleep away
the long & lonely afternoons
into half-remembered dreams.

Off from the kitchen where books & teas & apples
press their smells into wooden shelves,
I have planted a garden & filled it
with scraps of poems & things that really grow.

I remember my mother sometimes
when I do not distract myself with other things
her eyes, the distance between our storms
& I wonder how she lived so long
after her death.

I have become a seed saver
to halt the tide of disappearance.
I write poems & sleep with sunflowers
to fend off the disease of womanhood.

you & I
we drain berry juice into the porcelain sink
sip tea & speak of rain.

karyn m. bruce

Nine Ways to Contemplate the Key West Cat

1.
Inhaling the cool, ocean breezes
I am mesmerized
by the red-painted toe nails
of the café waiter
and the twitching of whiskers
beneath my chair.

2.
I take my map
and check it carefully.
Each cat is historically
landmarked.

3.
I would rather
pay my dues to Hemingway
by sitting with his cats
in the afternoon sun
than by pretending
I appreciate his words.

4.
Counting stars
or counting paw prints along these sidewalks:
I do not know which is easier.

5.
I detour along the path
toward the City Cemetery
to photograph the graves
and the hollow eyes
of waking cats.

6.
It is all the same:
the writers who write
then write of the writers
who have written here
and that cat
chasing its own tail.
It is the cat
which holds my attention.

7.
Shadows thicken.
Through dusty courtyards
cats linger
waiting for scraps of music
to fill the empty night.

8.
The sun is setting.
A cat must be singing.

9.
Oh, tourists on Duvall Street!
Do you not have dreams
of a brown cat
dreaming she is a cat
dreaming?

The Simple Truth

I am sixty-six years old. I know this
because I have a birth certificate, and every once in awhile
I see a face in the mirror I don't recognize.
My granddaughter asked me once what the wobbly skin is
underneath my chin and I had to stop and think. Oh yeah,
that. I have never looked or acted my age. Not even now.
I'm not even sure what that is. Age. I am me. I have a life.
I have owned it, trashed it, spilled it out like spoiled milk,
mopped it up, trampled it, breastfed and coddled it.
I have feared loving it; feared not loving it.
But it breathes, nonetheless.
I remember the wrinkled Greek grandmother who lived
behind my house. Every day she took a towel and swatted
the mosquitoes on her garage. She sang her songs
and thwacked those mosquitoes for hours,
delighted with herself. I pitied her, but what is the difference
between murdering a mosquito and writing a poem?
It's what she did. It's what I do. No pity; no shame.
A word. Once it's on the page, it is dead. Used up.

Like a mosquito splattered on a garage wall. Like life.
I never thought about dying until I had a life I wanted to
keep. I believe there's a heaven, but I also believe I will lose
enough weight to fit back into the "other side of the closet"
clothes. I like being. I want to be here. Not in a book of
dead poets. Not stuck in *Ancestry.com* . Not a word or a
smashed up bug. My father left me with a curse.
"All our 'family' die in their sixties." And he died
from a stroke three weeks after he turned sixty-seven.

The simple truth is I am nearing his death age. It has come
when I least expected it. Like a sun shower. Or a flat tire.
Here it is. I'm not sure I know what to do with it. Or not.
Years ago, a friend and I made a deal that whoever died first
would have to find a way to let the other know
there really is life after death. He went first. Wrote a note in
the clouds. "I c u." And I cried more over that than his
death because, now, I should probably believe, right?
If I am alive after my 70th birthday, well, then,
I will still be alive, and, more than grateful for it.
If not, I'll just be another daughter. mother. grandmother.
Who died.

Karyn M. Bruce is a native of Michigan. She wrote her first poem when she was 12, and won her first poetry award in eighth-grade.

A graduate of Bowling Green State University, Ohio, she has a BFA in Creative Writing and she has both M.A. and Educational Specialist degrees from Barry University, Miami Shores, FL. A middle-school English teacher for 18 years, Karyn is currently a freshman English professor at Johnson & Wales University.

I Will Write Loudly So You Can Hear Me is Karyn's second published book of poetry, the first being *Through Every Season Bright and New*, which she wrote for her daughter. She and her husband live in Miami, FL, with two cocker-spaniels, Lillie and Lucie, and a cat named Tree.

www.ingramcontent.com/pod-product-compliance
Lightning Source LLC
Chambersburg PA
CBHW031316060726
47590CB00003B/1237